A Pianist's Debut

A Pianist's Debut

Preparing for
the Concert Stage

by Barbara Beirne

Carolrhoda Books, Inc. • Minneapolis

Enormous thanks go to Leah and her grandmother Kyung Choi. What a treat it was to work with them and learn about the world of music through them! In addition, this book would not have been possible without the support of two special people—Debra Kinzler of The Juilliard School and Mary Bozanic of the Children's Professional School. I'm grateful for their help. There are many others to thank. Ana Berschadsky, Ann Van Voorhis, Marion Mundy, and Penny Pollock read the text and made wonderful suggestions. Nancy Wilson and Richard Rodzinski of the Van Cliburn Foundation and the photographers from the White House graciously provided me with the materials I needed. My family warmly supported me through this two-year project—as did my enthusiastic and talented editor, Marybeth Lorbiecki.

The photographs on pages 7 (top) and 8 have appeared through the generosity of Leah and Kyung Choi.

LIBRARY OF CONGRESS CATALOGING-IN-PUBLICATION DATA

Beirne, Barbara.
  A pianist's debut : preparing for the concert stage / by Barbara Beirne.
    p. cm.
    Summary: An eleven-year-old piano student describes her early interest in music, her first piano competition, her experience of moving with her grandmother from Los Angeles to New York to attend The Juilliard School of Music, and her aspiration to become a concert pianist.
    ISBN 0-87614-432-6 (lib. bdg.)
    1. Yoon, Leah—Juvenile literature. 2. Pianists—United States—Pictorial works—Juvenile literature. [1. Yoon, Leah.
  2. Pianists.] I. Title.
ML3930.Y66B5 1990
786.2′092—dc20   90-2238
[B]   CIP
[92]   AC MN

Manufactured in the United States of America

1 2 3 4 5 6 7 8 9 10 99 98 97 96 95 94 93 92 91 90

My son, Chris, has always felt his life would be
incomplete without music. This book is for him.

My name is Leah Yoon, and more than anything else, I want to become a concert pianist.

I'm 11 years old, and I'm studying music at The Juilliard School in New York City. The music conservatory here is one of the best in the world. Pianist Van Cliburn, violinist Itzhak Perlman, and cellist Yo-Yo Ma all studied at Juilliard. I'm hoping that if I work hard enough, someday I'll have a career making music too.

I'm not from New York. I grew up in Los Angeles, California. I lived there with my grandma who is raising me. We had an upright piano in our living room, and I started playing it when I was two years old. But as much as I begged, Grandma wouldn't let me take lessons.

"You're too young," she'd say.

Grandma did paint letters on the piano keys though. I learned that each sound a key makes has a letter to match it. Grandma called this ear training.

When I was five years old, I started taking piano lessons at the Colburn School of the Performing Arts. But I had a big problem. My legs were so short I couldn't reach the pedals. Grandma had to buy a special piano attachment called a pedal extension, which fit over the pedals and made them easier to reach.

After a year of piano lessons, my teacher, Ms. Hwang, entered me in my first competition. About 15 children played in my division. I don't know how old they were, but all of them looked pretty big to me. I played my favorite piece, a sonatina by Friedrich Kuhlau. At the end when the judges presented the awards, I was surprised. I'd won first prize! The judges gave me a large trophy.

Because of the competition, the Young Musicians Foundation heard about me. They gave me a scholarship for my piano lessons, and when I was eight years old, they invited me to play in a special concert.

Nick Vannoff, a television producer, came to listen, and he liked my performance. Afterward he asked me if I would like to play at the Kennedy Center in Washington, D.C. I said yes, of course.

The invitation was a huge honor. I was going to be playing in one of the most important concert halls in the United States. And to make everything even better, Grandma, Ms. Hwang, and I were invited to the White House for a reception before the concert.

It's hard for me to remember much about the
reception because I was so jittery about my performance. But I do remember meeting President Reagan.
He could only talk to us for a few minutes. Even so,
he made me feel very comfortable. The White House
photographers took pictures of us with the president
and Mrs. Reagan. They also photographed Grandma
and me in front of the White House Christmas tree.

Then came the performance. I'll never forget it.
The audience at the Kennedy Center was huge. I
played a solo piece with the Opera House Orchestra,
and the audience applauded loudly. I remember
thinking, "Wouldn't it be great to be a concert
pianist!"

The performance at the Kennedy Center inspired me to work even harder than I had been. Every day after school, I played the piano for four hours. My goal was to become a student at the world-famous Juilliard School. I thought that if I could make it there, I would become a concert pianist for sure.

But Grandma didn't think it was a good idea. She worried about things. She said that since I was only 10, I was too young for a move like this. She was afraid we'd be lonely in New York City, where we didn't have any relatives or friends.

After talking about it for weeks and weeks, Grandma finally said we could go. We took a trip to New York, and I played for some judges at The Juilliard School. They awarded me a full scholarship. I'd made it!

Grandma went job hunting right away and found a job at a beauty parlor near the school. At the end of the school year, we moved from Los Angeles to New York City. We were both a little scared.

The move was hard. Grandma and I lived in a furnished room for three months while we looked for an apartment near the school. We got lost a few times.

Until we were settled, I didn't have my own piano. I had to wait for a practice room at Juilliard. That often took a long time, since the rooms are usually full.

I was relieved when we finally found an apartment. And a piano. Grandma bought it secondhand.

Now I spend each Saturday from 9:00 A.M. to 6:00 P.M. at The Juilliard School. My program, the Pre-College Program, is for musicians who have not yet graduated from high school. Some of my classmates are only nine years old.

My first class is Chorus. Ms. Scott, the voice coach, tells us that singing and playing the piano are similar. When you sing, you have to control your breath so that you breathe only at the end of each singing phrase. If you breathe at other times in the music, it's like putting a period in the middle of a sentence. Your song will sound choppy, or it won't make sense.

Playing music on an instrument works the same way. Musical pieces are often divided into phrases, and if you breathe in the middle of a phrase, the sound and feeling of your music will change.

Solfège is my next course. Solfège is a French word, and it means using *do, re, mi, fa, sol, la,* and *ti* to sing musical notes. Our teacher, Ms. Thompson, has us sing musical pieces we don't know by sight-reading them. We read the notes on our sheet music and sing without stopping. It's hard to do, but it trains our eyes to move quickly. We learn to connect the notes and rhythms on musical scores with the sounds they represent.

At other times, Ms. Thompson plays music on the piano, and we try to write down the notes she has played. It's very much like the ear training Grandma taught me.

Chamber Music is another course we all have to take. Chamber music is music written to be performed by a small group in a person's home or in a small concert hall. In my chamber-music group, Rebecca plays the violin and Debbie plays the cello.

Playing in a music group is like playing on a baseball team. You have to depend on the other team members. If one musician doesn't play well, the music sounds terrible. So we learn to listen closely to each other and depend on each other's abilities.

Our teacher, Ms. Goldberg, says that this team effort will help all three of us "to expand our reach artistically." I think she means that we'll try harder because we don't want to disappoint our friends.

Another important course is Repertory Class. I take this from my Juilliard piano teacher, Ms. Carlson. In her class, everyone takes turns playing piano pieces. As one person plays, the others listen and watch carefully. Later we comment on the performances. Playing in front of an audience like this is good practice for our recitals at the end of the year.

To help me in my studies at Juilliard, I have a tutor named Mr. Kay. We often talk about music theory. He explains to me how chords and rhythms are put together and how other parts of music work. These things are difficult to understand, and sometimes it's almost like learning a foreign language.

   At The Juilliard School, there is a feeling of intense
competition between the students. We all know that
only a few of us will ever make it to the concert stage.

Lately I've been watching some of the advanced
students prepare for major competitions. My friend
Eduardus Halim has applied for the Van Cliburn
Competition in Fort Worth, Texas. He says that at
least 250 pianists from 37 countries will apply to
compete. Only 40 will be chosen. Everyone wants to
be selected because the competition's winner will be
invited to play on a long concert tour.

Someday, if my dream comes true, I'll be accepted
for the Van Cliburn Competition.

Each Saturday when classes are over, I go to meet Grandma at the beauty shop. On the way, I look at all the billboards. The Juilliard School is part of Lincoln Center for the Performing Arts, and a lot of concert halls are also part of the center. It's fun to see what's going on and who's playing. One day I want to look at a poster and see my name in big letters!

At the beauty parlor, I wait for Grandma to finish. She has to work long hours. It's expensive to live in New York City.

If Grandma isn't too busy, she trims my hair while I tell her about the day's events. Sometimes she laughs when I get too intense or frustrated about my piano playing. "You have to learn to be more patient, Leah," she says.

When the beauty parlor closes, we walk home.
We always go past Lincoln Center. The fountain and
twinkling lights are so pretty. In the winter, there's
a Christmas tree in front of the Metropolitan Opera
House. The lighted tree makes the center look even
more beautiful.

During the week, I go to the Professional Children's School. This is a regular school where I study English and Math, and other subjects that are required. The thing that's different about my school is that all the students here are preparing for careers in the arts. Some are already working in their fields. The hallways are filled with photographs of students who are actors, dancers, musicians, and models. Sometimes I see classmates on television.

I'm glad this school gave me a scholarship. No one here treats me as if I'm different because I spend so much time at the piano.

My best friend at PCS is Jenny Somogyi. Jenny is a ballet dancer who studies dance at the School of American Ballet. Sometimes we meet after school for ice-cream cones. This is a treat, since most afternoons we have to rehearse or practice.

I love to hear Jenny talk about her dancing. She was chosen to be one of the "garland girls" in the ballet *Swan Lake* at the Metropolitan Opera House. She tells me how on opening night, Mikhail Baryshnikov, the famous dancer, watched the girls rehearse.

"That's very good," Mr. Baryshnikov said. "But a little more glide, girls, a little more glide."

Every day I practice the piano for at least five hours. I get up at 5:30 A.M. and practice for two hours before school. Then, in the afternoon, I practice from 3:00 P.M. to 6:00 P.M.

Before beginning I warm up my hands by playing scales. Then I try a piece I'm comfortable with. After I've worked for a while on things I know, I start on a new piece, always trying to build up my speed and dramatic intensity.

Practicing is not something I *have* to do—it's something I *want* to do. I love music. I'm happier when I'm playing the piano than at any other time. Some nights I can hardly believe it when Grandma says it's time for dinner.

Pianists have to be very careful of their hands when they practice. Once, after a long stretch of hot and humid weather, the wires on my piano tightened, and the keys were hard to play. I strained my fingers. The doctor said that I had to stop playing the piano for two weeks. It was a long, lonesome 14 days. I felt as if I'd lost my best friend.

Thursday is Grandma's day off. It's also the day I have a private lesson with my piano teacher Ms. Gray. Before we start, Ms. Gray and I usually talk about the piece of music I'm going to play. She says that it's important to understand the feelings the composer was trying to communicate, because I have to express these feelings to the audience through my performance.

Today I'm going to play "Kind Im Einschlummern," by Robert Schumann. The English translation is *Child Falling Asleep.* Robert Schumann loved to write musical compositions about his children. In this piece, Schumann wanted his listeners to picture how beautiful a baby looks drifting off to sleep. When I play this piece, I think of my little cousin Mary in her crib. I play the notes softly, as if I'm trying not to wake her.

Ms. Gray is pleased with my interpretation, but she makes some suggestions about my playing.

"Remember your posture, Leah," she says. "Be a queen at the piano."

Ms. Gray has been a concert pianist herself. She stresses posture because when you sit with your back straight, you have the best possible reach and control of the keyboard. Good posture also helps you breathe properly.

Ms. Gray ends the lesson by assigning Beethoven's *Pathétique* Sonata. The music looks so difficult it makes me dizzy.

The weeks pass with the same schedule—practice, school, private lessons, and Saturdays at Juilliard. One week I take a break from my usual routine to work on the 75th Anniversary Benefit for the Professional Children's School. The benefit is going to be held at a large club. At least 500 guests are coming for dinner and a musical show.

I'm going to sing in the chorus with my friends. Ms. Gray says it'll be a good experience for me. I'll be able to practice communicating to an audience without a piano in front of me.

On the day of the benefit, classes are cancelled, and we rehearse all day. Everyone is excited. There'll be a party after the show, and we all wonder what to wear.

During a break, some friends say, "What about playing a little jazz, Leah?" They're surprised when I tell them I don't have the slightest idea how to play jazz or rock music.

That night I wear a dress Grandma made for me, and Grandma wears her beautiful green-and-silver dress. This is the special dress she wore to the White House reception. Since Grandma was born in Korea, she likes to wear her traditional Korean dress for important occasions.

My friend Chrissie McDonald and I arrive at the club early to look over the dining room. A lot of reporters have come to cover the event. A radio interviewer comes up and talks to Chrissie and me. The reporter asks us if it's hard going to school and preparing for a career at the same time.

Chrissie answers, "It sure is. Sometimes I get really tired and can't finish my homework." I add that I think it's hard too. Just last week I had to miss Jenny's birthday party.

The performance begins, and the audience loves the school chorus. We sing before the soloists, who are all people who once went to the school.

The only student performing a solo is Midori. She is a famous concert violinist. Midori has played with symphony orchestras all over the world, and sometimes she tells us about her experiences. She says that luck plays an important part in anyone's success.

When Midori was 14, she performed with the Boston Symphony at the Berkshire Music Festival in Massachusetts. The night she played was very hot and humid. In the middle of her performance, her E string broke. Midori quickly took the concert master's violin and continued playing. Just a few minutes later, another E string broke! She had to use a third violin.

At the end of Midori's performance, the crowd cheered, and the conductor, Leonard Bernstein, hugged her. The next day, an article about Midori came out on the front page of the *New York Times*. Midori claims that luck and the two broken strings helped her become recognized as a serious performer.

Midori's life is so exciting. It's the kind of life I want to have someday.

As soon as the benefit performance is over, I slip back into my usual routine. It won't be long now before my first New York recital. I can hardly wait.

Fortunately Grandma loves music as much as I do. When we have any free time, we go to concerts or other musical events.

One afternoon we attend a Master Class at Juilliard.
At the class, Lev Vlasenko critiques the performances
of five advanced students. Mr. Vlasenko is a well-known
pianist and teacher from the Soviet Union. As he talks
to the students, the rest of us listen. He tells them:

Play with personality!
Take risks.
Put more of yourself into the music.
Do not be afraid.
Play with confidence.

I'm going to try to remember these suggestions for
my recital.

Finally Ms. Gray gives me the good news. It's time to begin working on my recital piece. For the performance, Ms. Gray assigns me a work from Bach's *The Well-Tempered Clavier*. To learn more about my new assignment, I go to the New York Library & Museum of the Performing Arts, which is part of the public library at Lincoln Center. The library has a huge music department.

A copy of the original score of *The Well-Tempered Clavier* is in the research section. I check it to make sure the notes in my score are correct. I also take out some books that tell me about the piece. The word *clavier* means keyboard, and *well-tempered* refers to a system of piano tuning used in the early 18th century.

Then I find a surprise. Beethoven practiced *The Well-Tempered Clavier* when he was 12 years old. That really makes me feel good, since I'm only 11.

The library has many musical recordings, and I'm able to listen to famous pianists play my recital piece. It's interesting to hear other musicians' interpretations. But I never, never try to imitate them. I want to develop a style of my own.

My favorite concert pianist is Alicia de Larrocha. She has a light and feathery style. When I was younger, I used to worry that my fingers would not grow long enough to reach certain chords. But then I discovered that de Larrocha has small hands. She said that having small hands made her learn to use her "musical imagination." Since many times she couldn't use other pianists' ways of fingering, she had to come up with her own ways of reaching for certain chords or notes. This makes her playing sound different from other pianists'.

I try hard to use my musical imagination. I experiment with various ways of playing until I'm perfectly happy with the sound I make. Sometimes I strike the keys harder or softer, or I use the pedals differently, or I try new fingerings.

During the weeks before my recital, I practice every free minute. But Grandma and I take time off to look for a new dress. It seems everything we see is too sophisticated or too babyish. Then we find a pink dress that seems just right.

At last, the night of the performance arrives!

I wait in the wings until it's time to go onstage.
There's a little hole in the stage door where you can
peek out and watch the audience. My turn is coming
up, so I take one last look at the score—but it's hard
to concentrate. It seems like forever before the
stage manager says, "You're on."

I walk out on the stage trying to look as calm and confident as possible. As I adjust the piano bench and sit down, I remember my teacher's words: "Be a queen."

Something happens when I start to play. A calm feeling comes, and I forget about the audience. It's almost as if I'm playing in my own living room.

I play my last note, and there's a silence.

Suddenly the applause starts. It goes on for a long time. I don't think I've ever felt happier than I do now. I want to shout, *HOORAY!* But instead I bow with as much dignity as I can.

When the recital is over, I rush to find Grandma.
She gives me a hug and a beautiful bouquet of flowers.
   I'm so lucky! I get to do what I love most—MAKE
MUSIC.

I think the most important thing for young people going into classical music is that they must love it more than anything in the world. They must feel that without it their lives would be incomplete and that they have to have it at all costs and at all expense for the rest of their lives.

Van Cliburn